PUFFIN BOOKS

UK | USA | Canada | Ireland | Australia | India | New Zealand | South Africa

Puffin Books is part of the Penguin Random House group of companies whose
addresses can be found at global.penguinrandomhouse.com.

www.penguin.co.uk   www.puffin.co.uk   www.ladybird.co.uk

Penguin
Random House
UK

First published 2025

001

Text copyright © Maddie Moate, 2025
Illustrations copyright © Paul Boston, 2025

The moral right of the author and illustrator has been asserted

'I Like To Move It', © Strictly Rhythm Records Inc, 1993, published by Strictly Rhythm Publishing (page 16)

All opinions are the author's own or those of experts. The author has taken
great care to check factual accuracy and secure permission to use expert content.

The information in this book is intended as a general guide and is believed to be correct as at March 2025.
The author and publishers disclaim, as far as the law allows, any liability arising directly
or indirectly from the use or misuse of any information contained in this book.

Printed in China

The authorized representative in the EEA is Penguin Random House Ireland,
Morrison Chambers, 32 Nassau Street, Dublin D02 YH68

A CIP catalogue record for this book is available from the British Library

ISBN: 978–0–241–65255–8

All correspondence to:
Puffin Books, Penguin Random House Children's
One Embassy Gardens, 8 Viaduct Gardens, London SW11 7BW

MIX
Paper | Supporting
responsible forestry
FSC® C018179

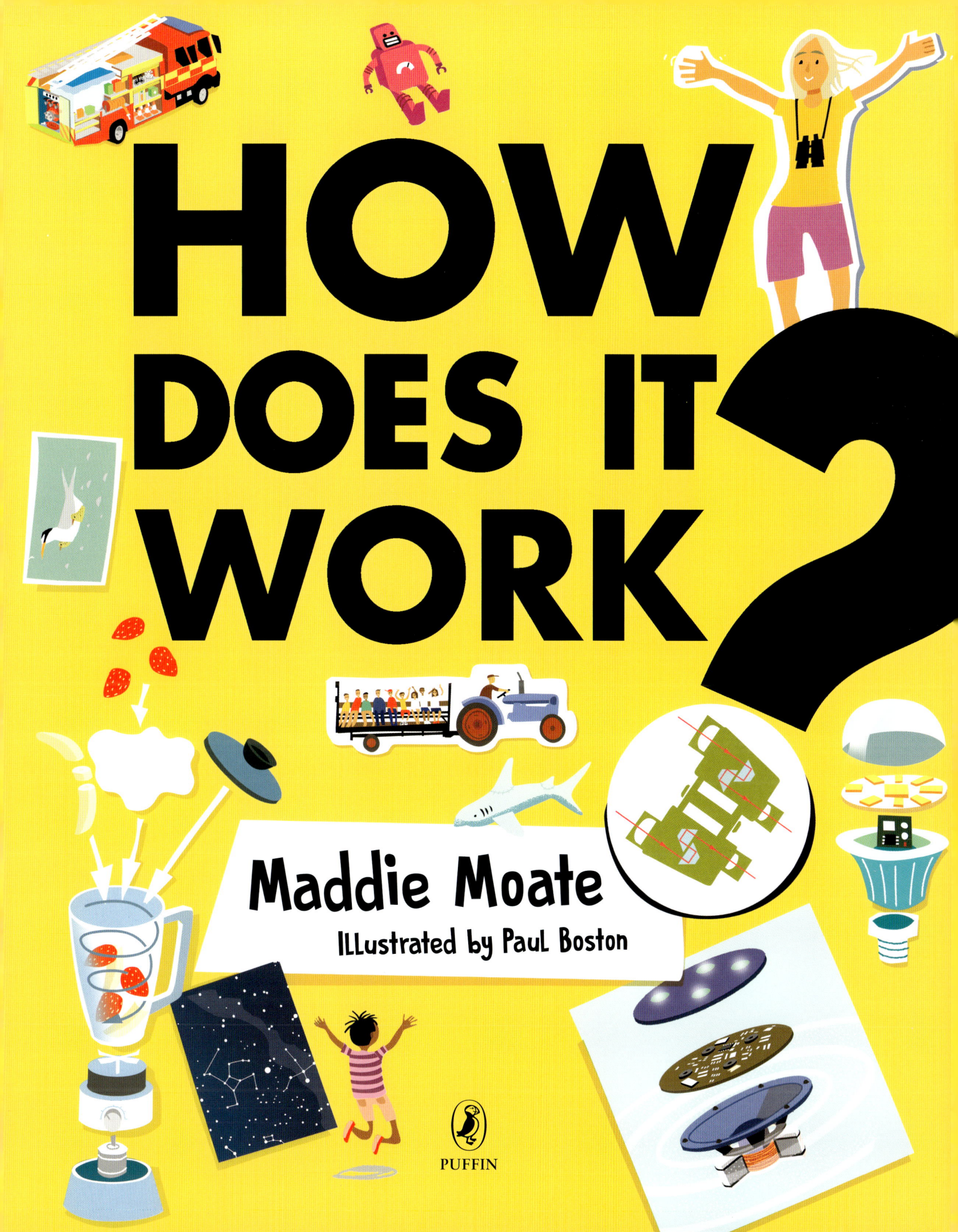

HOW DOES IT WORK?

Maddie Moate

Illustrated by Paul Boston

PUFFIN

Hi, I'm Maddie!

I'm so pleased that you've picked up my book. If you've seen the title (which you probably have), then I reckon you might be curious to find out how things work. I know I am!

Every day, we use all kinds of objects, machines and technology, and I'm constantly asking . . .

'How does it work?'

Dishwashers are brilliant (less washing-up for me!), but what happens when you close the door?

How does a digital camera capture a moment and piece it back together on a screen?

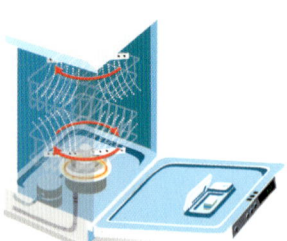

And what about binoculars? They make tiny, faraway things look HUGE! Is it some kind of magic? No, it's science!

In this book, I've set out to find answers to these questions and many more. And my favourite way to learn about the world and all the things in it is by going on adventures.

An adventure doesn't have to mean travelling to faraway places. You can go on adventures in your local area, with your friends and family, and even in your own home. Adventures can be big or small – all you need is a big dollop of curiosity.

As you turn the pages of this book, we're going to go on four adventures, each with its own mission. While learning how everyday things around us work, we'll also be searching for hidden objects, spotting differences, solving mazes and helping with puzzles.

Sounds fun, right?

On page 8, our first adventure begins. My nieces and nephew have come to stay, and we're going to have a race with a remote-controlled car. But first, you need to help me find some missing parts!

What are you waiting for? Let's get started!

Stay curious,

Maddie

CONTENTS

Useful Things to Know

To help you understand how the objects and machines described in this book work, there are some things you might want to know on pages 56–57, which may be helpful to flip back to as you travel through each adventure.

Whenever you see a word highlighted Like this, you can find a definition for it on pages 58–59, while words that look **like this** will pop up in diagrams.

You'll also find the answers to each of our adventure puzzles on page 60.

Finally – there are lots of hidden details on every page, so see how many you can spot in my 'Things to Spot' on page 61!

RACE AROUND THE HOUSE

Today we're going to have an epic race in the garden with my remote-controlled car. But there's a problem: the car is missing some of its parts! They could be anywhere – the kitchen, bathroom, bedroom, or the lounge . . .

I need you to help me find the missing pieces and put them back together. Can you spot where the car is hiding?

Bathroom

Bedroom

Kitchen

Lounge

9

Breakfast Time

Good morning!
It looks like a bright, sunny day – perfect for our race.
If only we could find the car . . .
But first, let's have some breakfast. I like to start with
a glass of cold orange juice straight from the fridge.

Fridge

How does the fridge keep our food cold?

It's all thanks to a clever cooling liquid called **refrigerant** that gets pushed around by a special pump called a **compressor.**

First, the cold refrigerant is pumped through tubes inside the fridge called **evaporator coils**, which take in heat from the air, cooling it down.

As the refrigerant collects heat, it warms up and **evaporates** – turning from a liquid into a gas, which then flows back to the compressor.

Sometimes I make a smoothie for breakfast – my favourite is strawberry and banana!

Refrigerant

Evaporator coils

Condenser coils

ACHOO!
It's dusty back here!

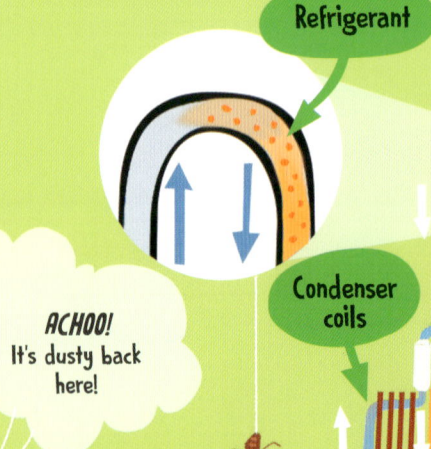

The compressor pushes the gas particles together, making them **vibrate** and get hot. The hot gas is pumped towards tubes called **condenser coils.**

The condenser coils are at the back of the fridge, where it is cooler, so the hot gas **condenses** back into a liquid. This then flows back to the evaporator coils for the cycle to start again.

Compressor

Blender

Let's start by putting all the ingredients in the **jar**.

Strawberries

Banana

Milk (dairy or plant-based!)

Screw the **lid** on tight and press the start button.

The **electric motor** spins the **blades**, which chop up the chunky ingredients and mix them with the milk and air.

Jar

Lid

The blades on a blender are very sharp, so you should always make smoothies with a grown-up.

Everything whizzes round in a spiral movement, like a whirlpool! The mixture is pushed up the sides of the jar, so any big bits can fall towards the blades and get chopped up really small.

This creates a deliciously frothy, smooth liquid. Enjoy!

Blades

Electric motor

What a delicious breakfast! Let's be helpful and put our dirty cups and plates in the dishwasher to get them sparkling clean.

Dishwasher

Inside the dishwasher are **racks and a basket** that hold our plates, bowls, cups and cutlery.

In the **door**, you'll spot the **detergent (soap) dispenser**. This is for the dishwasher tablet or detergent.

When the dishwasher is full, you press the start button on the **control panel** and close the door.

If you listen, you might hear a *CLUNK!* This is the dishwasher tablet being released from the dispenser.

Racks and basket

Water inlet

Spray arms

Water pours in through the **water inlet**. Then the **heating element** warms it.

Heating element

Pump

Drain pipe

Door

Motor

Detergent dispenser

Control panel

An electric **motor** powers the **pump**, which pushes the soapy water through a pipe and out of tiny holes in the spinning **spray arms**.

Water spurts on to the dishes and washes away all the grease and food.

Finally, the dirty water is drained away, and fresh water is pumped through to give everything a rinse.

You found the remote-controlled car! But we still need to find its missing wheel. Let's visit the bathroom to brush our teeth and see if we can find it . . .

Car

Smile!

Did you know your teeth are covered in the hardest material in your body? It's called *enamel* and it's harder than gold, silver and even iron! But it can still get damaged if we don't clean our teeth regularly. So, let's get brushing.

Toothbrush and Toothpaste

When bits of food get stuck between your teeth, they can become a tasty meal for tiny living things called *bacteria*. These release *acid*, which can make little holes in our teeth called *cavities*.

But brushing your teeth with toothpaste helps to scrub away this acid, strengthen enamel AND leave your breath smelling fresh!

Toothpaste

Toothbrush

Sink

What's in toothpaste?

Fluoride helps strengthen enamel.

Abrasives are tiny gritty bits that polish your teeth.

Detergents make toothpaste foamy when it gets mixed with water.

Flavours make toothpaste taste nice!

Now, where has that wheel got to? Could it be in the toilet?

After all, the toilet does make things disappear – poo, wee and toilet paper!

Toilet

A toilet has two main parts: the **cistern** and the **bowl**. When you press the **flush**, it moves a lever, which lifts the **flapper** out of a hole at the bottom of the cistern.

Clean water rushes into the toilet bowl, pushing the water with your wee, poo and toilet paper through a bendy pipe at the bottom called a **U-bend**.

When everything has been flushed away, air travels up the U-bend and makes a gurgly sound!

GURGLE

Flush

Cistern

Bowl

Flapper

U-bend

When the cistern is empty, the flapper closes and clean water flows back in, ready for the next time the toilet is flushed!

Soap

Don't forget to wash your hands!
Ooh, that hand soap smells nice . . .

Our skin makes oil to keep it soft and healthy. But if we don't wash often, the oil builds up and can attract dirt and bacteria.

Water isn't good at washing away oil because water and oil **molecules** don't mix. But soap molecules have one end that loves water, and another end that is attracted to oil.

(Molecules are made from **atoms** – the tiniest particles that make up everything in the universe. A molecule is made from two or more atoms stuck together.)

Soap molecule

When you mix soap with oil and water, one end of the soap molecule sticks to the oil and the other end sticks to the water. As you rinse the water away, all the dirt, oils and soap go with it!

Hot Water

Usually a combination boiler has a **primary heat exchanger** that heats water for your radiators, and a **secondary heat exchanger** that heats water for your taps.

Oof, that water is COLD!
I need it a bit warmer to wash my hands.
But how does the water get hot?

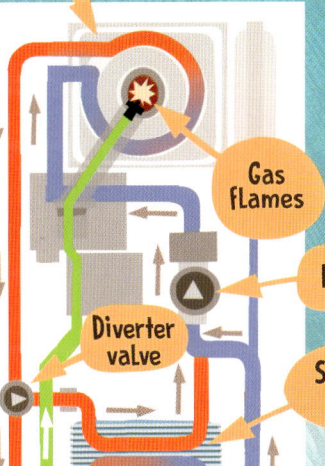

Primary heat exchanger

Gas flames

Pump

Diverter valve

Secondary heat exchanger

Cold water in

Hot water out

Gas

The primary heat exchanger is heated by a small row of **flames**. The secondary heat exchanger is heated using hot water from the primary one.

When we turn on the hot tap, the **diverter valve** sends hot water into the secondary heat exchanger to warm it.

The cold water inside the secondary heat exchanger gets hot and is sent through pipes to your hot **tap**!

Tap

Bathtub

This cycle starts again every time you need hot water.

You found the missing wheel! But hang on, we're missing the transmitter that controls the car.

Let's look in the bedroom. But please close the door behind you. I just need to – ahem – use the loo.

Back to Bed

Ooh, it's lovely and cosy in here. Now, where is that transmitter?

Lamp

Most bedside lamps have three main parts: a **power source**, a **lightbulb** and a **switch**. These parts are connected by **wires** to make an *electrical circuit*.

Electricity only flows round a circuit with no gaps. When the switch is open (off), it makes a gap in the circuit. When the switch is closed (on), it completes the circuit and electricity can travel round it, lighting up the lightbulb!

But how does the bulb light up?

Radiator

Radiators are normally connected to a boiler by a set of pipes.

Hot water flows in through the **inlet valve** and heats the air that passes between the radiator's front and back **panels** and hollow **flutes**.

This creates a circular movement of air, as warm air rises up and away from the radiator, while cooler air sinks down and is heated again. So the room slowly heats up!

I should turn the lamp on. It's hard to see in this corner of the room.

LED Lightbulb

Flutes

Panels

Switch

Power source (plug socket)

Wires

Most bulbs used today contain **LED chips**, which last a really long time. LED stands for 'Light Emitting Diode'.

Lens

LED chips are small electronic devices with a special *semiconductor* material inside. This material gives out lots of light when electricity flows through it!

Return pipe

LED chips

Eventually, the hot water inside the radiator cools down, so the **return pipe** collects the cooled water and carries it back to the boiler for reheating.

Inlet valve

Duvet

When it's cold outside, it's lovely to snuggle up under a duvet. Have you noticed how they start cool and slowly warm up?

Duvets are stuffed with a fluffy filling, such as feathers or polyester (a type of plastic). It feels squashy because of air pockets between the strands of material. When you're in bed, your body heat warms the cooler air inside the duvet and gets trapped!

Trapped warm air

Fibres

The temperature of the air close to your skin gets warmer, in a process called *insulation*.

Glow-in-the-dark Stars

Wow, these glowing stars look super-cool in our dark fort! But how do they work?

Most glow-in-the-dark stars are made by mixing materials called **phosphors** into melted plastic, which is then moulded into shape.

Phosphors soak up energy from light sources and VERY slowly release this energy as light in another colour – usually a spooky green – in a process called **phosphorescence**. This weak light can only be seen in the dark – so we call it 'glow-in-the-dark'!

It's not just ceiling stars that give off a magical green glow. You might have glow-in-the-dark stickers, pyjamas or even a remote-controlled car!

Perhaps the transmitter is under the covers?

Bedsheets are also great for making a cosy fort!

Transmitter

The glow-in-the-dark stickers helped us find the transmitter! But it's not making the car move. A-ha – it's missing its batteries! Let's look for them downstairs . . .

Lounging Around

Let's stick some music on and boogie while we look for those batteries!

Smart Speaker

A smart speaker uses both hardware and software, which work together to make it . . . well, smart!

When you say the wake word, the **microphone** captures the sound. The software recognizes the wake word and activates the virtual assistant – the part of the software that understands your commands. Our virtual assistant is called Ada.

The virtual assistant connects to the internet and replies through the speaker.

Hey there, Ada.

Ada, please can you play – 'I Like To Move It'?

Sure, here is 'I Like To Move It'.

Inside the speaker is a **cone,** which is like a tiny drum attached to two **magnets.** When the smart speaker plays, the magnets push and pull each other. This moves the cone back and forth quickly, which creates a *sound-wave*.

Sound-waves are made by air molecules bumping into each other and creating a chain of vibrations. When these vibrations reach our ears, our brain translates them into sound.

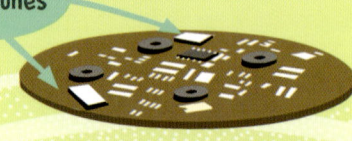

Microphones

Cone

Sound-waves

Magnets

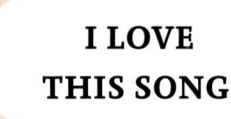

I LOVE THIS SONG!

16

ADA, STOP

PHEW! I'm exhausted after all that dancing.
I think I need a sit-down.
Ooh, my favourite programme is on!

Television

When the television is turned off, the **screen** is black. But when we press the 'on' button, the **remote control** sends an instruction to the screen and a picture appears!

The screens on televisions, smartphones and tablets are all made up of thousands of tiny squares called **pixels!**

Each pixel is made of three different coloured lights called **sub-pixels**. They are red, green and blue.

Pixels

Sub-pixel

When all three lights are turned down, the pixel looks black. But when they are turned up or down to different levels, they can create millions of different colours.

Screen

Remote control

If we focus on just one pixel while watching TV, we'll see the sub-pixel lights constantly change colour – like a mini disco!

But if we zoom out and watch the full screen, all the colour-changing pixels work together to create moving pictures – a bit like a moving mosaic!

Batteries

We need two batteries, so why don't we just take them from the remote control?

Woohoo! Finally we have everything we need to make the remote-controlled car work. Let's head outside and play!

Garden Games

What perfect sunny weather for our race! Our friends have come to join in the fun.
Now we have all the parts we need. But do you know how a remote-controlled car works?

Transmitter
(the remote control)

Remote-controlled Car

A remote-controlled car is controlled using a transmitter, but for both to work, they need some power, which usually comes from **batteries**.

When you press a button on the transmitter, it sends a message to the car through invisible waves called *radio waves*.

Radio waves send signals by changing the way they wiggle back and forth. When we want to send an instruction – such as telling the remote-controlled car to move left or right – we press a button. This makes the transmitter change the pattern of wiggles in the radio waves.

Axle

Motor

Receiver

Batteries

Inside the car, there's a tiny **receiver** that recognizes the patterns in the radio waves and understands the messages being sent. When it gets the message, it tells the **motor** to turn the **axle** and spin the wheels, so the car goes in the direction we want it to!

Can you think of any other devices that use a remote control?

Here's the racetrack I set up in the garden.
Can you work out the quickest way to reach the finish?

THE BIRTHDAY-PARTY DASH

Supermarket

MUNCH!

House

I'm off to a birthday party, and you're invited! It's at the community farm, where there's lots of animals AND a playground. But first, we have some jobs to do. We need to go to the supermarket, bake a birthday cake and find my camera to take photos of the party.

Now, where did my camera get to?
Can you see it anywhere?

Farm

Playground

Great Picnic Spot

21

Supermarket Sprint

The super-awesome birthday party List

For the picnic
Carrots
Bananas
Sausage rolls
Popcorn

For the cake
Flour
Butter
Eggs
Sugar
Bicarbonate of soda
Strawberries
Double cream

Our first stop is the supermarket.
I've written a shopping list for some picnic food –
I hope they have everything we need!

Let's get a shopping trolley –
luckily I have a coin to unlock one.
But how does it work?

Lock mechanism

PLastic bar

Coin

Side arms

Bolt

TroLLey Lock

When we push a **coin** into the trolley **lock**, it separates two **side arms** and pushes a **plastic bar** down. This releases the **bolt** connecting the trolley to the one in front. We slide the bolt out to unhook the trolley.

When we're done, we use another trolley's bolt to get our coin back. Pushing the bolt into the lock squeezes the two side arms together, and the plastic bar pops back up. This holds the bolt in place and our coin pings out!

Clever, isn't it? The coin works like a key, and it reminds us we have to return our trolley when we are finished.

Well done, we've got everything on our list! Let's load the shopping on to the conveyor belt and pay at the checkout.

Hi, Sam!

TILL No.3

Belt

Emitter sensor

Motor

Roller

Receiver sensor

Roller

BEEP...

BEEP...

BEEP...

Conveyor Belt

A conveyor belt is made up of a wide plastic **belt**, tightly stretched round two or more **rollers**. A **motor** spins them, causing the belt to move round in a looping motion.

But what if we've got LOADS of shopping? How does the belt stop everything from piling up at one end?

At the scanner end of the conveyor belt is a set of sensors. The **emitter sensor** sends out a light beam that shines into the **receiver sensor** opposite.

When an item passes through the sensors, the beam of light is broken. This sends a signal telling the motor to stop. When the item is picked up to be scanned, the light can shine across again, restarting the conveyor belt.

Can you see what Sam is scanning? It looks like a TINY zebra crossing. It's called a barcode.

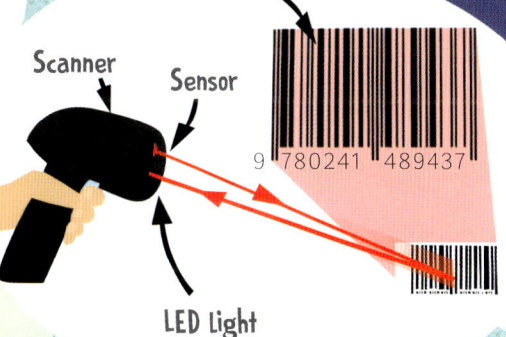

Barcode

Scanner

Sensor

9 780241 489437

LED Light

Barcode

The **scanner** shines a red **LED light** on to the barcode, which reflects back into a **sensor**.

The white stripes reflect lots of light, while the black stripes reflect less. The scanner captures this pattern and translates it into numbers. The white stripes are recorded as **0** and the black stripes are recorded as **1**.

This is called a binary code, which the computer turns into a 13-digit barcode number.

100100 11011010100
000100 1000100101
00101 011011 001001
101 001000 1001000
1010 01001 1 01001
00 101 011000 101000

£1.40

The computer has thousands of barcode numbers stored in its memory and each number matches an item.

When the computer matches the barcode number with an item in its *database*, it tells us what it is and how much it costs.

Once all the barcodes have been scanned, the computer can add up the cost of our shopping.

Now it's time to go home and turn all this lovely food into a birthday picnic! I hope you like baking . . .

Let's Bake!

It's time to get baking for our birthday celebration!
But how do we turn the ingredients into a delicious fluffy cake?

Cake Mixture

We measure out the cake ingredients and mix them in a bowl.

Whisk whisk whisk

Then we pour the mixture into a tin and carefully place it in a hot oven (with our oven gloves on!).

The heat gives the ingredients energy so *chemical reactions* can take place. These transform the sloppy mixture into a bouncy sponge!

But what does each ingredient do?

Bicarbonate of soda helps the cake to rise. As the mixture is heated, it releases bubbles of gas that get trapped inside, making the cake fluffy and light.

Flour contains long, chain-like molecules called proteins. When heated and mixed with liquid, protein molecules make a stretchy gloop called *gluten*, which helps trap the bubbles of gas.

Egg also contains tangled-up protein molecules, but when heated, those chains untwist and make a firm structure like a net. This also helps to trap bubbles of gas and hold the other ingredients together.

Butter coats the other ingredients with a greasy layer, which stops them drying out when they're heated in the oven.

Sugar makes our cake taste nice and sweet but also keeps it moist, as sugar particles attract and hold on to water molecules.

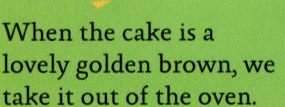

When the cake is a lovely golden brown, we take it out of the oven.

Finally, let's whip up the double cream and slice the strawberries to make a delicious topping!

Now that our cake is ready, let's prepare some snacks for our picnic. We can use the air fryer to warm up our sausage rolls!

Air Fryer

An air *fryer* is a confusing name, because it doesn't *fry* food with oil. Instead, an air fryer uses air to heat our food and cook it.

First, we place our sausage rolls on the **grate** inside the **frying drawer**.

Next we set the cooking temperature and timer using the buttons on the **control panel**.

The **heating element** heats the air inside the frying tray. A spinning **fan** blows that hot air all around your food.

Whirrrrrrr

Yummy!

Because the sausage rolls are raised on the grate, the hot air can blast them from all sides, cooking them throughly and making the pastry nice and crispy!

Control panel
Fan
Frying drawer
Heating element
Grate

Microwave

Did you know that popcorn was the first food to be tested in a microwave? (The second food to be tested was a boiled egg . . . but it exploded. So please always ask a grown-up to help you with any kind of kitchen gadget.)

Inside the microwave is a device called a **magnetron** that changes electricity from the power socket into special waves of energy called microwaves.

The magnetron sends the microwaves through a metal tube called a **waveguide**.

They bounce off the metal walls of the **cooking cavity**, where food spins on a **turntable**. The microwaves hit the food from all directions, cooking it evenly.

The microwaves cause the water, fat and sugar molecules in the food to wiggle around and vibrate.

The vibrating molecules let out heat, which cooks your food from the inside!

Cooking cavity
Waveguide
Magnetron
Control panel

POP!
POP!

Door

Turntable

Our birthday picnic is ready and it's time to head to the community farm. I wonder what animals we'll see?

Welcome to the Farm!

Let's go and say hello to the birthday boy, over by the rabbits. We're ready to take some photos!

Look – Snuffles the rabbit is having a drink. Her bottle is upside down, so why isn't she getting wet?

Plastic bottle

Bottle cap

Metal tube

Metal ball

Sipper Water Bottle

It's because there's a secret **metal ball** hidden inside the **metal tube**.

When Snuffles licks the end of the tube, it pushes the ball up. This makes a little bit of space for air to get in and a drop of water to get out.

When there is air in the tube, water gets pulled from the bottle to fill the empty space. This means Snuffles can drink drop by drop.

If Snuffles stops drinking, the ball settles in the bottom of the tube, making a seal. This closes the gap, so no more water can drip out.

Mehhhh!

I'm wearing my favourite cardigan today. It's soft and warm because it's made from a special material – wool!

Wool

Wool is the name given to hair or fibres that come from sheep – as well as goats, alpacas and camels! It's used to make hats, socks, jumpers, cardigans . . . and even our picnic blanket!

Sheep wool keeps us warm because its curly fibres trap pockets of air that get heated by our bodies. And sheepskin produces lanolin: a greasy wax that protects the sheep's wool from the rain and helps keep them (and us!) cosy and dry.

In the spring, farmers use clippers to gently trim off the wool, so the sheep can be cool in the summer before growing a new coat for next winter. This is called **shearing**.

The wool coat that is cut from the sheep is called a fleece and it's HEAVY.

A fleece can weigh around 15 kilograms – that's as much as fifteen bags of flour!

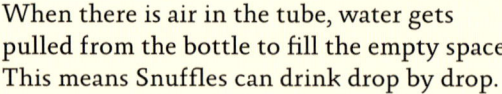

Tractors

Tractors come in all sizes and colours. This green one has chunky back wheels with deep ridges called **treads** to help it pull heavy things across the muddy farm. Here are a few of the different machines a tractor can pull!

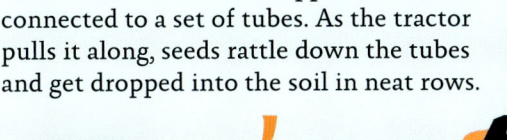

Front Loader: This is used for grabbing, lifting and moving heavy things like soil, stones and hay.

Moldboard plough: This machine cuts, lifts and loosens soil ready for planting seeds.

Seed drill: This has a hopper full of seeds connected to a set of tubes. As the tractor pulls it along, seeds rattle down the tubes and get dropped into the soil in neat rows.

Rotary mower: This uses spinning blades to trim crops and grass, like a big lawn mower!

Trailer: A tractor's trailer can move animal feed, bales of hay and even people around the farm!

Treads

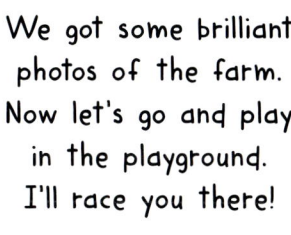

The wool is taken to a mill, where it's washed to get rid of any bugs, twigs, grass or poo that might be stuck to it!

Once it's clean the wool is passed through a carder, which gets rid of any knots – just like a big comb.

Lastly a big spinning frame turns the fibres into long threads called yarn, which people can use to knit with.

We got some brilliant photos of the farm. Now let's go and play in the playground. I'll race you there!

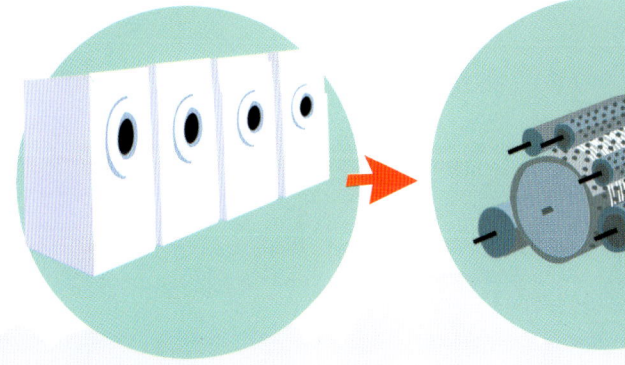

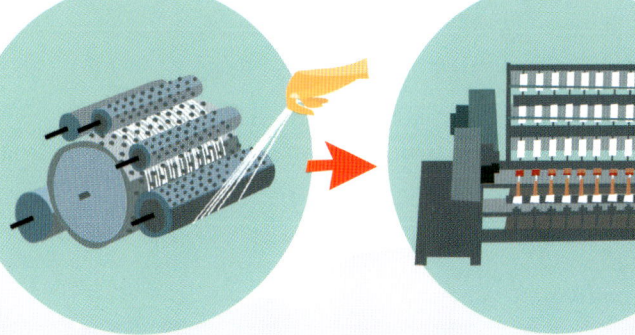

Playground Party

You win! Phew, that was fast . . .
Let's have a go on the seesaw –
I could do with a sit-down!

Seesaw

A **force** is a push or pull on an object. You use force to push down on a seesaw, which makes the other end pop up.

The bar of the seesaw acts as a lever. This is a simple machine that helps lift or move objects when a force is applied at one end.

The central point that the lever balances on is the **fulcrum**.

We call the force pushing down at one end of the lever the **effort**, and the weight at the other end the **load**.

If one end of the seesaw weighs more than the other, the load will be greater than the effort, so that end will tip downwards.

That's why sometimes we need to use our feet to push off the ground – this creates enough effort to lift up the load at the heavier end, before it tips back down again.

Boing! Boing!

Hey, you two! Say cheese!

Effort

Load

Fulcrum

But if two people of the same weight sat on a seesaw without using their feet, it would balance in the middle!

Slides

A slide is a super-fun way to get from somewhere high up . . . to somewhere lower down. *Weeee!*

The reason we slide down a slide is because of an invisible force called *gravity*.

Earth's gravity pulls everything down towards the centre of the planet. Without gravity, things would just float about!

Sometimes we slip down a slide super-fast, and other times really slooooowly.

This is because of another force called *friction*, which happens when two objects slide past each other. It makes them slow down and get hot!

Slides are made of smooth, slippy materials like plastic, because these create less friction than bumpy ones.

Our clothes also affect our speed and the amount of friction on a slide.

Someone wearing a slippy superhero costume would be a lot faster than someone in a ballet tutu with wellies.

But the grippy wellies would help them to climb back up again!

Gravity

If you feel your bum get a bit hot when you're on a slide – that's friction in action!

Roundabout

A roundabout has a spinning base with a handrail attached to it. When someone pushes on the handrails, it spins round and we have to . . .

Hold on tight!

Wahoo!

Roundabouts are lots of fun, but they can make us feel *really* dizzy! Why is that?

It's because of something happening deep inside our ears. Did you know that your **inner ear** controls your balance as well as your hearing?

Inside your inner ear, next to the snail-shaped **cochlea** – which is a bit like the ear's microphone! – there are three tiny loops called **semicircular canals**.

These canals contain tiny hairs called **cilia** and are filled with fluid. When you move around, the fluid moves too, and the cilia send signals to your brain to tell you which way you are moving. When you stop, the fluid stops moving and the cilia tell the brain that you are now still.

Semicircular canals

Cilia hairs

Cochlea

Outer ear

Eardrum

Inner ear

When you spin round on a roundabout, the fluid in your inner ear sloshes about in circles. When you suddenly stop spinning, the fluid keeps moving about for a little while.

This creates a confusing muddle of signals for your brain, which makes you feel dizzy!

Friction

All this birthday fun has got me feeling hungry. I think it's time we enjoyed our picnic!

Picture Perfect

The picnic looks SO tasty. Let me take a quick picture before we tuck in! *CLICK*
Have you ever wondered how a digital camera works?

Digital Camera

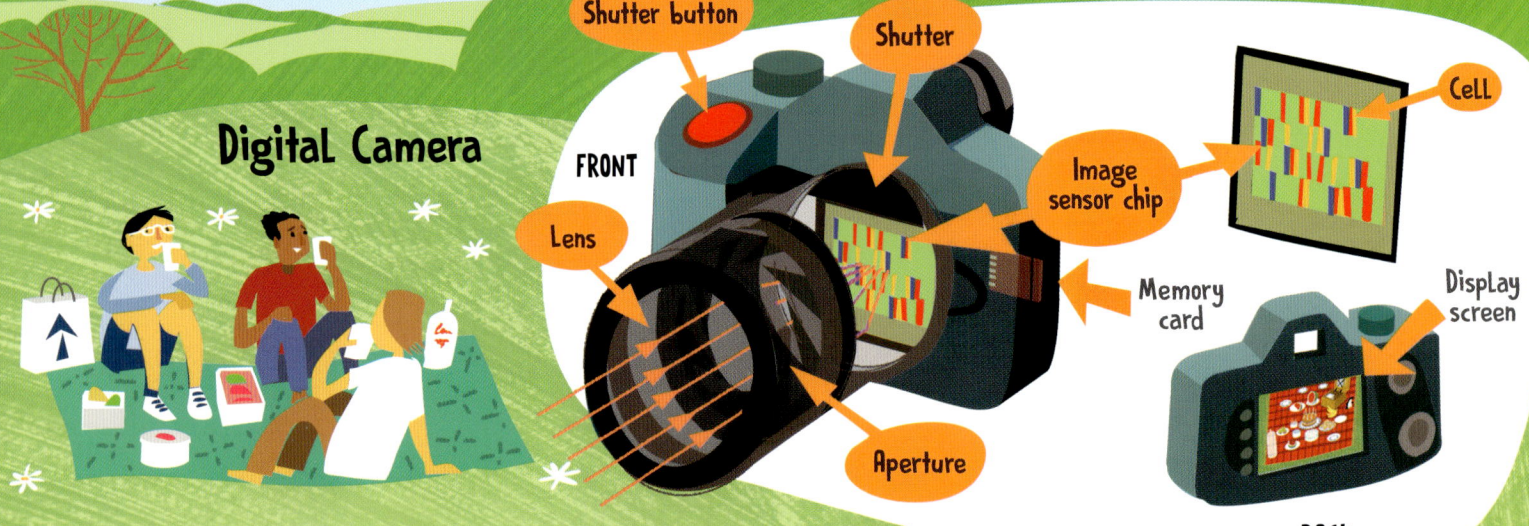

Shutter button
Shutter
Cell
Image sensor chip
Display screen
FRONT
Lens
Memory card
Aperture
BACK

You press the camera's **shutter button** to open the **shutter**. It's a bit like the camera's eyelid! It lets light enter the camera's **aperture**, just like our eyelids let light into our eyes. The camera only needs a quick burst of light to capture a photo, so the shutter opens and closes like a fast blink.

With the shutter open, light streams into the camera through a special piece of moulded glass called the **lens**.

When light rays pass through the curved lens, they bend towards a single point or *focus*. This directs the light rays on to the **image sensor chip**.

If you zoomed in, you'd see this chip is covered in tiny blocks called **cells**. These cells are good at sensing light and can even measure its colour and brightness.

The image sensor chip works super-fast to turn the light energy into electrical signals. These are turned into a digital code that the camera saves on its **memory card**, where the photos are stored.

When it's time to see your photos, a computer can use the digital code to recreate the image by piecing it back together on the **display screen** – like a digital puzzle!

CLICK

The camera in a smartphone is made up of the same key parts as a digital camera – a lens and an image sensor – but on a much smaller scale!

The display screen at the back of the camera lets us take a quick peek at our photos. But if we wanted to see them a bit bigger, we could plug the camera into a laptop or computer screen. (To learn how screens work, go to the TV on page 17!)

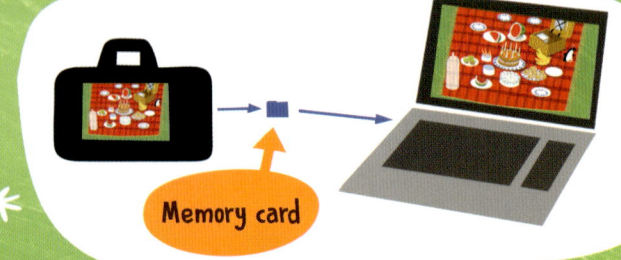

Memory card

Spot the Difference

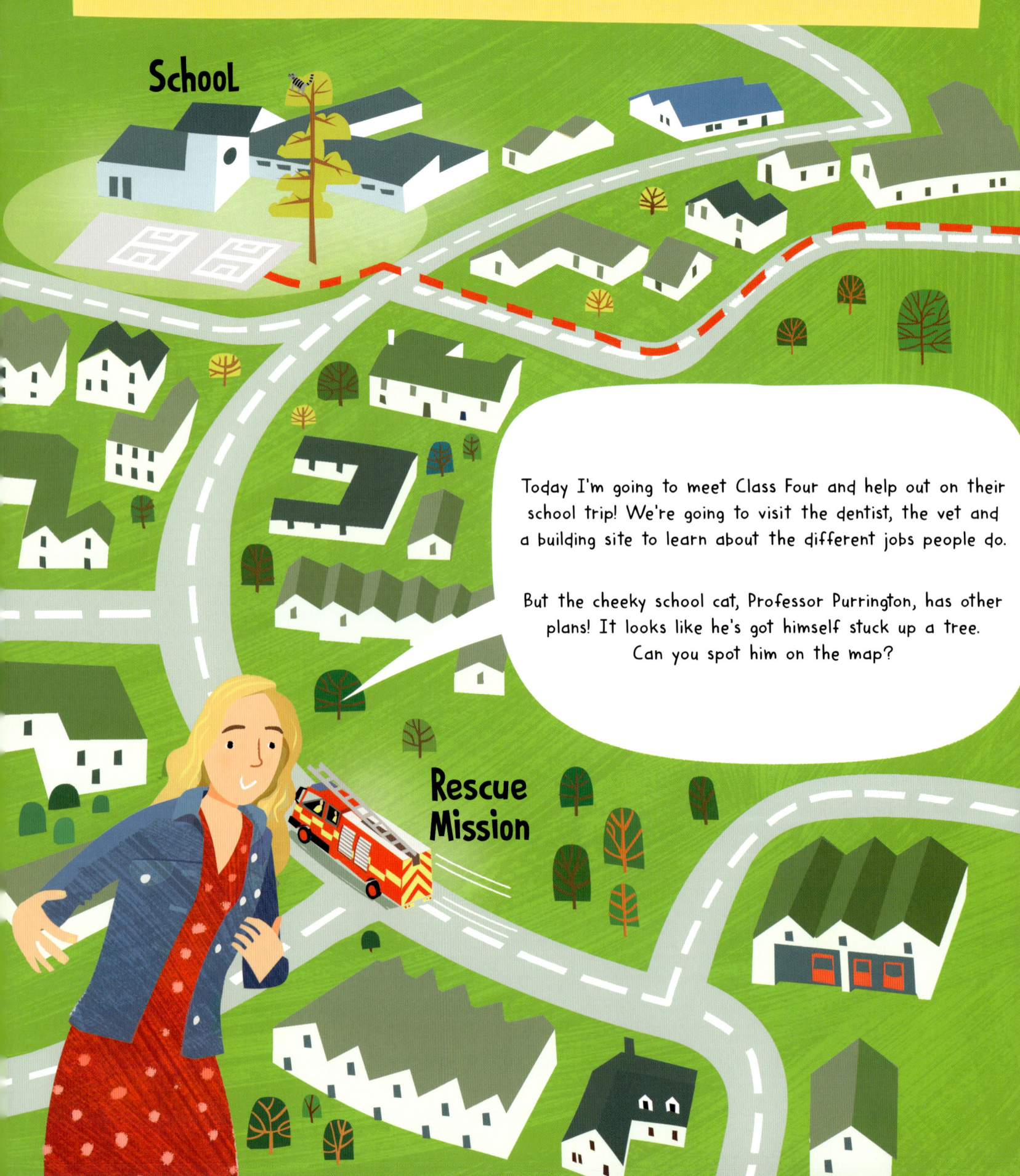

Dentist

Vet

Building Site

33

A Classroom Commotion

We'll be heading off on our trip as soon as Ms Maple finishes her science lesson. She's writing on the board using a marker pen. But how does the pen work?

Professor Purrington

Marker Pen

Inside the **barrel** of a marker pen is the **ink reservoir** – a spongy tube soaked in liquid **ink**. The pen tip is made with **felt**, which has tightly packed fibres with narrow gaps between them.

The water molecules in the liquid ink like to stick together. But they are even MORE attracted to the narrow gaps inside the felt. This attraction pulls the first water molecule up into the felt tip, and it pulls the other water molecules along with it!

When the felt tip has soaked up enough ink from the reservoir, we can use the pen to draw on paper or a whiteboard!

We call this movement *capillary action*.

Capillary Action

Felt tip

Barrel

Ink

Ink reservoir

Stem

Leaves

Pea pod

Xylem

Water molecules

Roots

The class are growing peas from a pea-pod plant. Did you know the peas inside the pod are actually the seeds of the plant?

Plant

The **roots** of a plant soak up water from the soil, but how does the water travel up into the plant? By capillary action!

Inside the **stem** of a plant are tiny tubes called **xylem.** They are the plant's water transportation system.

The **water molecules** are attracted to the walls of the xylem, which pulls them into the plant. This is how water travels from the roots up to the **leaves**!

Look at the clock – it's nearly time to set off on our trip . . .

Classroom Clock

Face

Minute hand

Hour hand

Second hand

Movement

Circuit board

Microchip

Motor

Quartz crystal

Battery

Gears

Shaft

This classroom clock has a round **face** and three hands: the **hour hand**, the **minute hand** and the **second hand**. When the clock ticks, we see the second hand move a tiny bit every second.

1, 2, 3, 4 . . . tick, tick, tick, tick.

The minute hand moves once every 60 seconds – or one minute – and the hour hand moves once every 60 minutes – or one hour!

But how do the hands move at the right speed?

At the back of the clock is the **movement**. It's powered by a **battery** that sends a flow of electricity through a *circuit board* and into a tiny crystal called a **quartz**. This makes it vibrate an exact number of times per second.

A **microchip** counts the vibrations. When it gets to the number that equals one second, it releases an electric pulse.

These pulses power a **motor** that turns a set of **gears** – little wheels with interlocking teeth. Each gear is for a different hand.

The gears are connected to a rod called a **shaft** in the middle of the clock face, which spins the hands at the right speeds!

Uh oh – Professor Purrington has got stuck up a tree again!

That curious cat . . . Please keep an eye on him while we're gone. Maybe we'll find someone to help on our trip!

Open Wide!

The dentist's chair might look like it belongs on an alien spaceship, but there's nothing to fear! It's a clever machine with special parts that help the dentist check your teeth.

Dental Chair

ME!

Hello, I'm Dr Bright. Who'd like to sit in my chair?

Dental Light

This helps a dentist see what they are doing. It can be moved around to light up your mouth.

Bracket table

This is used to hold all the tools a dentist might need:

Dental probe

A small metal rod with a pointy bit on the end. It's used to scrape away plaque – a sticky film of bacteria that can form on your teeth.

Foot pedal

The foot pedal lets the dentist move the chair into position.

Mouth mirror

This helps the dentist to see your teeth from all angles – even the back!

Air-water syringe

This is used to spray water or a tiny blast of air into your mouth to help clear saliva and get rid of any tiny bits stuck in your teeth.

Aspirator

This works like a tiny vaccum cleaner to suck up saliva that pools in your mouth when it's open wide.

The chair is a bit like a ride! It can go up and down, forward and back. But how?

Hydraulics

At the bottom of the chair is a special tube called a **hydraulic cylinder**. Inside it there is a **piston** – a metal rod that slides up and down.

When the dentist presses a button on the **foot pedal**, it switches on a **motor** that powers a hydraulic **pump**. This sucks in oil from the **oil reservoir** and pushes it out through a pipe. A valve opens to let oil flow into the hydraulic cylinder.

The oil pushes on the piston so it slides up and out of the cylinder, lifting the chair higher. When the chair is high enough, the valve closes, and the oil keeps the piston in place.

To lower the chair, the dentist pushes a different button on the foot pedal and a second valve opens to let the oil flow out. The weight of the chair pushes the piston back down again.

Piston

Foot pedal

Hydraulic cylinder

Motor   Pump   Oil reservoir

Look, I've got a wobbly tooth!

Wobbly teeth are perfectly normal. Let me explain . . .

Types of Teeth

When you are about five or six, your baby (or milk) teeth will start to wobble and fall out. As you grow and start eating tougher foods, you need a new set of bigger, stronger teeth!

An **adult tooth** starts to grow underneath and push on the baby tooth's root. As the **root** is worn away, the baby tooth gets wobbly and falls out! This leaves a gap for the adult tooth to push through your **gums**.

Molars help us to chew and grind our food.

Canines are sharp and pointy to help us tear our food apart.

Incisors have straight, sharp edges that work like a pair of scissors to cut our food.

Enamel

Baby (or milk) teeth

Dr Bright, Dr Bright! Did you know our cat is stuck in a tree?

Root

Adult tooth

Gums

Oh dear! Perhaps you could ask my friend Dr Barker at the vet's to help?

The root is the unseen bit that holds a tooth in place.

The gums are the pink fleshy parts round the bottom of your teeth.

At the Vet's

At the vet's, Dr Barker is showing the class how an X-ray machine works! She's taking an X-ray of Millie the puppy's broken leg.

X-rays

X-rays are a type of **radiation** – energy that moves from one place to another in waves. You have already learned about some types of radiation in this book!

We measure radiation on the **electromagnetic spectrum**.

At one end are long, low-energy waves:

Radio waves carry radio signals, WiFi and messages to remote-controlled cars.

Microwaves carry phone calls, heat our food and pop our popcorn!

Infrared waves are a type of energy wave we feel as heat. They can also be used to scan barcodes.

Visible light is light that we can see with our eyes, as well as through cameras and binoculars.

At the other end are short, high-energy waves:

X-rays are very powerful and can travel through materials that other waves can't. They can show us images of the inside of things, such as a bag at airport security, or the bones inside our bodies.

Stethoscope

A stethoscope is a special tool that allows doctors and vets to listen inside their patients' bodies. But how does it help the vet to hear?

RADIO WAVES   MICROWAVES   INFRARED   ULTRAVIOLET   X-RAYS   GAMMA RAYS

VISIBLE LIGHT

X-Ray Machine

An X-ray machine uses **X-rays** to take pictures of our bones, or sometimes our pets' bones! Although X-rays are safe for a short time, they can be dangerous for longer periods, so the vet needs to wear protective clothing.

Dr Barker places Millie on the **X-ray table** and turns on the **X-ray generator**. The X-rays can't pass through Millie's bones, but they do go through her skin and muscles, all the way to a **flat panel detector** below the table.

The flat panel detector turns the X-rays into digital signals that get sent to a **computer**, which creates an image on the **monitor**, or screen. The X-rays that couldn't pass through Millie's bones show up as white shadows.

X-ray generator

X-rays

Monitor

Computer

Flat panel detector

X-ray table

The white line shows where Millie broke her leg, but it's all healed now!

Before she can go home, I'm going to check her heartbeat to make sure she's healthy.

You might remember from page 16 that sound-waves are made by molecules bumping into each other and creating a chain of vibrations.

When Millie's heart beats, the vibrations create a sound-wave that travels through her body. When the vet places the **diaphragm** on Millie's chest, the sound-waves cause the surface of the diaphragm to vibrate too.

The sound-waves bounce off the inside walls of the **rubber tube**, travel through the **ear tubes**, into the **earpieces** – and finally up to the vet's ears.

Earpieces

Ear tubes

Diaphragm

Rubber tube

LUB, DUB,
LUB, DUB,
LUB, DUB

That's the sound of Millie's healthy heartbeat. She's all better now!

Excuse me, Dr Barker – please can we have some of these cat treats?

Of course! They should help you with your cat rescue operation . . .

We've got some cat treats, but we might need a ladder too . . .
Maybe we'll find one at our next location?

Can You Dig it?

A building site is a busy place with lots of machines and equipment. Charlie the site manager is here to show us around!

Digger

A digger is a helpful construction machine that can dig holes and move heavy loads.

The **bucket, dipper** and **boom** are controlled using **hydraulic cylinders** (like the ones we saw in the dentist's chair.)

Inside the **cab,** the driver pulls a set of **levers,** which change the length of the hydraulic cylinders. These move the boom, dipper and bucket to scoop up some earth.

Instead of wheels, the digger has a set of **tracks** – huge chains that move around in a loop.

Charlie

Dipper

Boom

Cab

Hydraulic cylinders

Levers

Sprocket

Rollers

Shoe

Idler wheel

Teeth

Bucket

The outside of the track is called the **shoe**. It has ridges that dig into the ground and stop the machine from slipping on muddy surfaces.

As the driver drives the digger, a wheel at the back of the track called the **sprocket** turns.

The sprocket's teeth lock into gaps in the chain that pushes the track around in a loop. This turns the large **idler wheel** and a set of **rollers**, which help move the track along and keep everything steady.

Concrete Mixer

Concrete is made by mixing water, sand, small stones and cement – a soft powder that becomes sticky when wet. Builders use a concrete mixer to keep the concrete wet so it can be poured. When concrete dries, it becomes hard and strong, perfect for building roads and laying bricks!

A concrete mixer is like a giant spinning barrel on wheels. First, the **drum** gets filled up with the ingredients.

Inside the drum is a special spiral **blade** that looks like a screw. When the drum starts spinning, the blade mixes all the ingredients together and drags the mixture towards the base of the drum.

If the concrete starts to dry out, the **water tank** can spray in some extra liquid.

When the spiral blade rotates in the *opposite* direction, it guides and pushes the concrete out of the drum.

Finally, the builders position the **chute** (like a slide for the concrete!), and the concrete can be poured where it is needed.

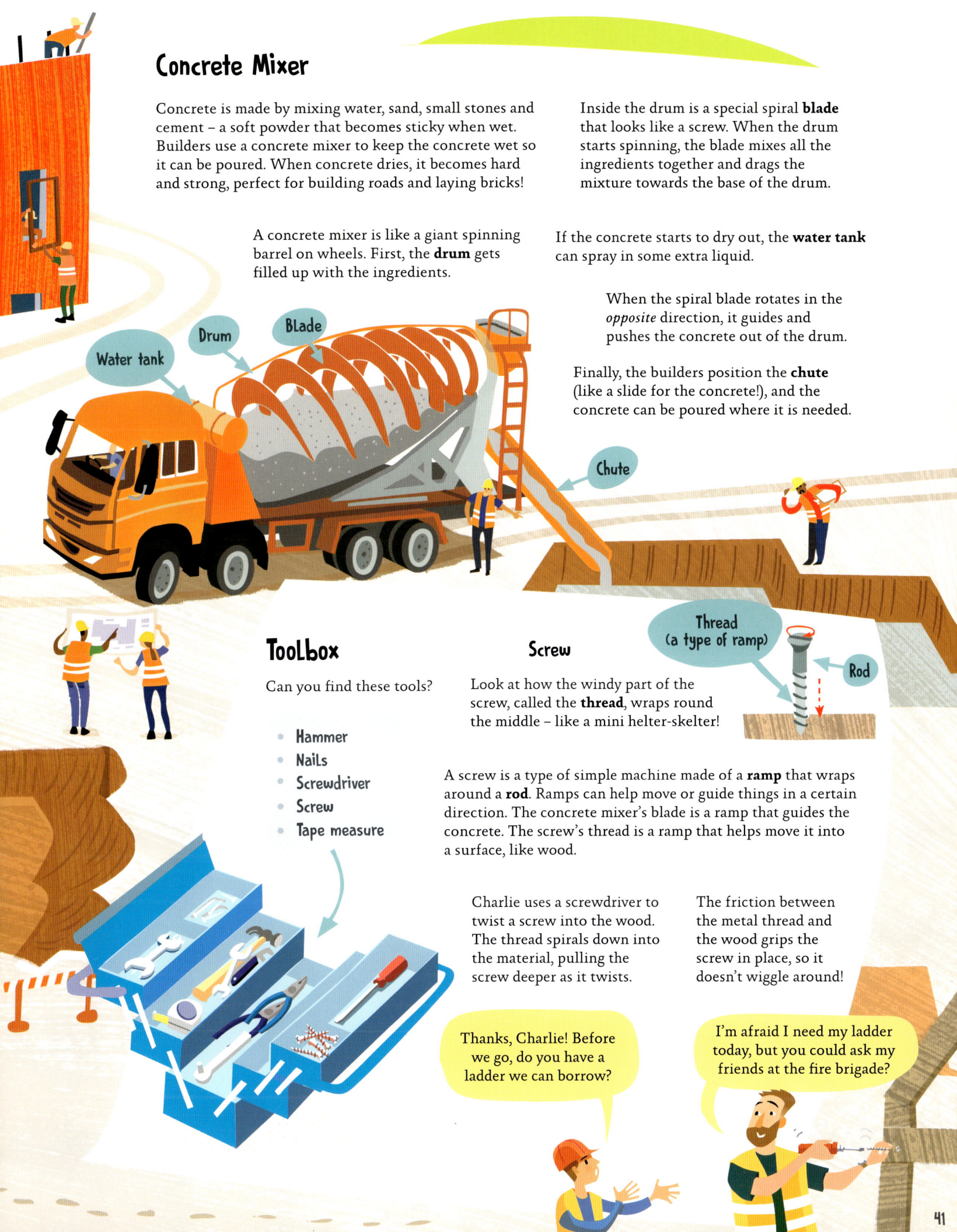

Water tank

Drum

Blade

Chute

Thread
(a type of ramp)

Rod

Toolbox

Can you find these tools?

- Hammer
- Nails
- Screwdriver
- Screw
- Tape measure

Screw

Look at how the windy part of the screw, called the **thread**, wraps round the middle – like a mini helter-skelter!

A screw is a type of simple machine made of a **ramp** that wraps around a **rod**. Ramps can help move or guide things in a certain direction. The concrete mixer's blade is a ramp that guides the concrete. The screw's thread is a ramp that helps move it into a surface, like wood.

Charlie uses a screwdriver to twist a screw into the wood. The thread spirals down into the material, pulling the screw deeper as it twists.

The friction between the metal thread and the wood grips the screw in place, so it doesn't wiggle around!

Thanks, Charlie! Before we go, do you have a ladder we can borrow?

I'm afraid I need my ladder today, but you could ask my friends at the fire brigade?

41

The Rescue Mission

Firefighters have to be ready for all kinds of emergencies, so their rescue vehicle is designed to carry lots of important equipment:

The fire-and-rescue service has arrived in their fire engine!

NEE NAWW NEE NAWW!

Ladders

Ventilation fan

Drone

First aid kit

Pump panel

Water tank

Pump

Hose

Traffic cones

Hose

How do fire engines pump water out of the hoses to put out a fire?

Impeller rotation

Water in

Impeller

Fire Hose

The fire engine's **water tank** can hold around 1,800 litres of water – enough to fill six bathtubs!

When they arrive, the firefighters unreel the hoses and attach them to the back of the engine.

The **pump panel** has levers and switches that control how much water flows from the tank and through the hoses.

A firefighter pulls a lever that lets water flow from the tank to the **pump**.

Water rushes into the pump and hits the centre of a spinning blade called an **impeller**, which flings it outwards. This pushes the water out of the hose really fast and really far!

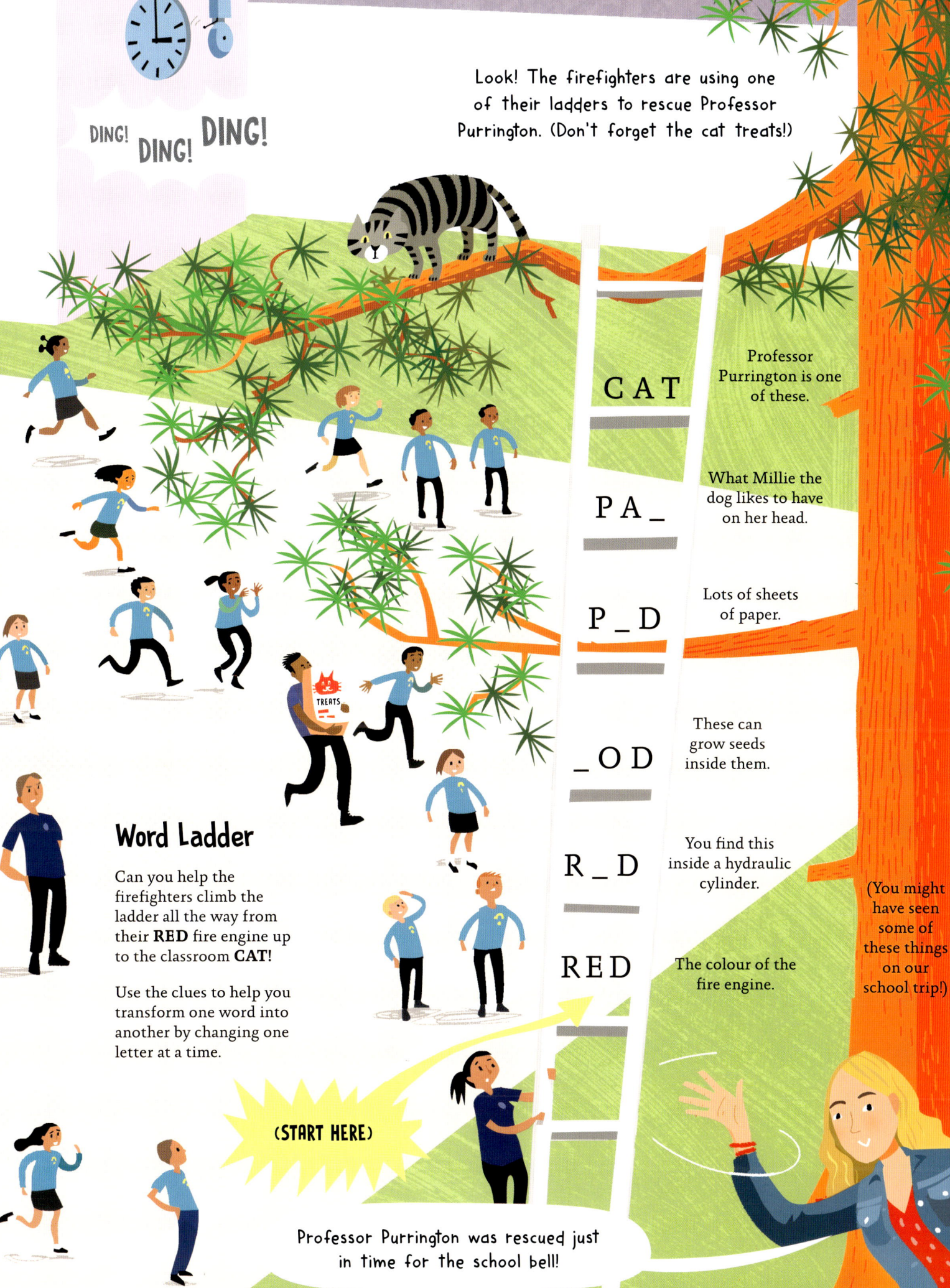

DING! DING! **DING!**

Look! The firefighters are using one of their ladders to rescue Professor Purrington. (Don't forget the cat treats!)

CAT — Professor Purrington is one of these.

PA_ — What Millie the dog likes to have on her head.

P_D — Lots of sheets of paper.

_OD — These can grow seeds inside them.

R_D — You find this inside a hydraulic cylinder.

RED — The colour of the fire engine.

(You might have seen some of these things on our school trip!)

Word Ladder

Can you help the firefighters climb the ladder all the way from their **RED** fire engine up to the classroom **CAT**!

Use the clues to help you transform one word into another by changing one letter at a time.

TREATS

(START HERE)

Professor Purrington was rescued just in time for the school bell!

THE GREAT HOLIDAY ADVENTURE

Home

Ferry Port

We're getting ready for a camping holiday. We'll travel by car and cross the sea on a giant boat called a ferry. How exciting!

I'm bringing my binoculars so we can get a really good look at everything we see on our trip.

Ferry Port

They make faraway things look bigger, so we won't miss anything when we're exploring.

I just need to find them first. Have you seen my binoculars anywhere?

Campsite

Beach

Hit the Road

We're packing up the car, ready to go!
Apparently, bicycles are the best way to explore the campsite,
so we're taking our bikes with us.
We need to charge up our electric car before we set off.
Some of its energy comes from the solar panels on the roof!

Pylon

Charger

Charging cable

Socket

Battery

Wheel

Electric motor

Electric Car

An electric car runs on electricity stored in a big **battery**. To charge the battery, we connect a **charging cable** from the **charger** to the car's **socket**.

This car's charger gets some of its electricity from the solar panels, and some from the *electric grid* – a network of power stations, cables and **pylons** that delivers electricity to our homes.

Now it's time to switch it on!

BEEP   Hummmmm

Unlike cars that burn fuel, electric cars hum quietly because they use an **electric motor** instead of a noisy engine.

When we switch the car on, electricity travels from the battery to the motor.

Solar Panels

Solar panels are made up of smaller sections called **photovoltaic cells**.

These cells are made of two different layers sandwiched together. The top layer is tightly packed with tiny particles called **electrons**.

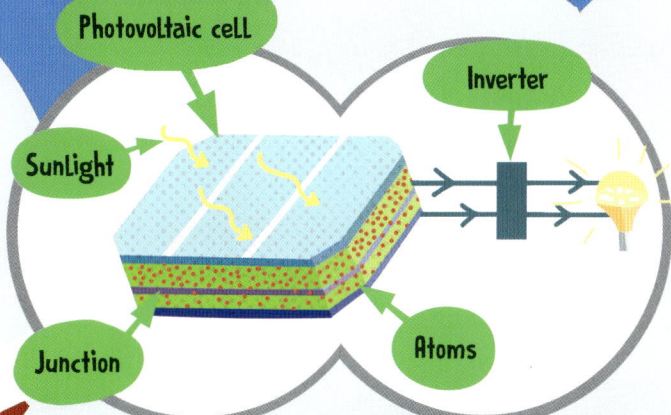

Photovoltaic cell

Inverter

Sunlight

Junction

Atoms

The bottom layer has fewer electrons with lots of gaps.

The place where the two layers meet is called the **junction**, and electrons can move across it.

Inverter

We can think of sunlight as a wave of tiny particles called **photons**. When photons shine on to the photovoltaic cell, they knock the tightly packed electrons in the top layer. This frees the electrons to move and cross the junction as they look for new gaps.

This movement makes a flow of electricity called an electric current, which streams out of the solar panel through a wire and into a piece of equipment called an **inverter**.

The inverter takes the electric current and turns it into the type of electricity that can power all the electronic things inside our home!

Some of the electricity made by the solar panels flows to the car charger on the side of the house.

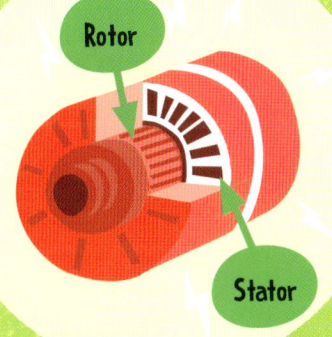

Rotor

Stator

The motor has two main parts: the **rotor** and the **stator**. The stator is fixed in place and contains a set of magnets arranged in a special pattern.

The rotor can spin round. It's full of thin, twisty metal wires. Electricity flowing through them creates a magnetic field – the area round a magnet that either pulls towards or pushes away magnetic objects.

When electricity flows into the motor, the stator's magnetic field starts to push and pull the rotor's magnets, which makes it rotate. The rotor is attached to the car's axles, so as they spin, the **wheels** spin too!

The car's packed up and it's time to hit the road!

Ahoy There!

How exciting – it's time to head off across the sea and start our adventure!
We're travelling on a ferry! A ferry is a boat that carries people
and their vehicles. But with all those heavy things on board, how does a ferry float?

Ferry

It's all thanks to *displacement* and *density*.

When you put something in water, it makes room for itself by pushing the water aside. This is called displacement.

The bottom of the ferry is super wide and deep, so it pushes aside a lot of water. The displaced water creates an upward force known as **buoyancy** that pushes back against the ferry, in the opposite direction to **gravity**.

If the weight of the water displaced is greater than the weight of the ferry, then the ferry will float!

Gravity

Buoyancy

So what about density?

An object's density depends on how tightly packed its **atoms** are. Things will float if they are either the same density or less dense than the water they are in. A ferry is made of heavy materials, such as steel. The atoms in steel are tightly packed together, so we say that it is dense.

However, a ferry also has lots of spaces inside it that are filled with air. The atoms in air are more spaced out, meaning air is less dense.

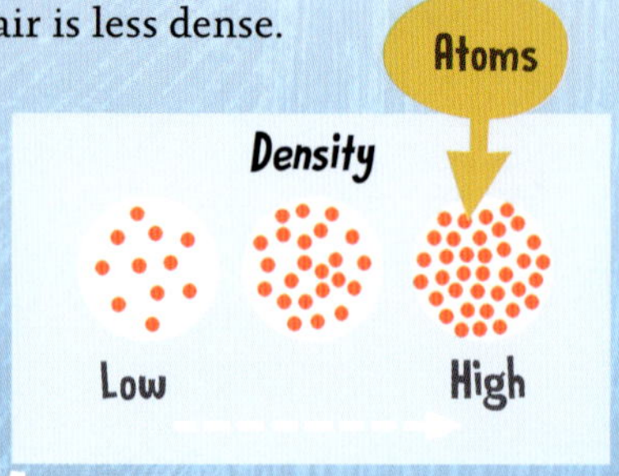

Although the ferry is heavy, the air-filled spaces make it less dense than the water. So it can float!

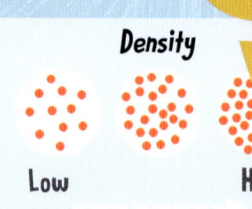

Atoms

Density

Low   High

48

Wind Turbines

It's super windy on the ferry. If you look in the distance, you can see lots of wind turbines! The offshore wind farm is making electricity for the electric grid. But how?

Wind turbines can be almost 100 metres tall. That's about the same as the Statue of Liberty!

At the top of the turbine **tower** are three long, propeller-like **blades**. The blades connect to the **nacelle** – the boxy bit at the top of the tower that moves to keep the blades facing the wind's direction.

The blades have a special curved shape that helps them 'catch' the wind. This pushes them round and round. The three blades fit into the **hub** (which looks like the turbine's nose!) and this is connected to a long rod called the **main shaft**. This turns when the blades rotate.

The main shaft enters the nacelle and goes through a set of gears. This speeds up the rotation, making a second shaft called the **high-speed shaft** turn much faster.

The high-speed shaft drives a **generator**. Inside it, the high-speed shaft spins **magnets** round a **coiled metal wire** that creates an electric current that can flow out of the wind turbine.

Blades

Nacelle

Hub

Offshore substation

Tower

Main shaft

High-speed shaft

Generator

Coiled metal wire

Magnets

The electricity zooms through undersea cables to a small building called an **offshore substation**. Here, electricity from all the wind turbines is collected and sent along a much larger cable to land, where it enters the grid and travels through power lines to get into our homes.

LAND AHOY! Next stop, the campsite.

49

Camping Out!

Welcome to the great outdoors! Before we explore,
we have to pitch our tent so we have somewhere to sleep.
But how does it fit inside such a small bag?

Camping Tent

A tent has parts that are small enough to pack away, but make something much bigger when put together.

Poles – These are often made with light, strong metals, such as aluminium. They have short sections that click together with the help of a stretchy elastic cord that runs through the middle. *BOING! CLICK!*

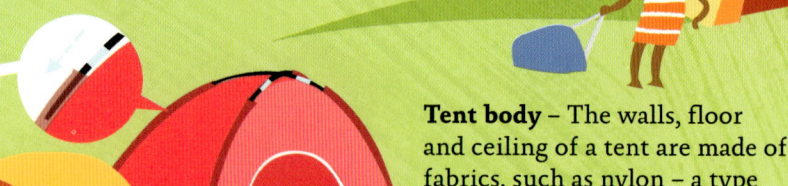

Tent body – The walls, floor and ceiling of a tent are made of fabrics, such as nylon – a type of flexible, tough plastic that can scrunch inside a small bag.

Guy ropes – Ropes attached to the outside of the tent that can be fixed to the ground with tent pegs.

Entrance – Most tent doors have a waterproof outer layer and a mesh inner layer with lots of tiny holes. This layer can be zipped close to help air flow in while keeping bugs out.

BUZZ!

Tent pegs – Small metal rods that fix a tent securely to the ground.

But how do you put it up?

1. Find a flat, clear spot. (Nobody wants to sleep on a slope or have pine cones poking their pillows.)

2. Lay the tent body flat and fix it to the ground with tent pegs.

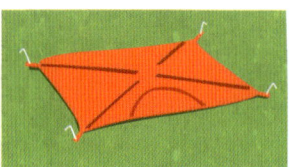

3. Build the tent poles by connecting the short sections together.

CLICK! BOING!

4. Thread the poles through the sleeves on the outside of the tent body. It's like sliding them into a fabric tunnel!

5. Lift the poles and bend them to make the frame. Each end of the pole fits into a hook at the bottom of the tent to keep it in place.

6. Tie down the tent by stretching out the guy ropes and fixing them to the ground with tent pegs.

Excellent job. Our cosy holiday home is complete.
Come on, let's go and explore on our bikes!

Bicycle

How do the pedals on a bike make the wheels go round?

Pushing the pedals turns a **large cog**, which is attached to a **chain** made out of smaller pieces called **links**. At the other end, the chain is attached to a **small cog** connected to the **back wheel**. As the large cog turns, its **teeth** hook into the chain's links and pull it in a loop, turning the small cog.

Back wheel

Small cog

Chain

Links

Large cog

Front wheel

Pedals

Teeth

When the back wheel turns, the **front wheel** is pushed along and the whole bike moves forward!

TWEET

Can you hear that?

Look, it's a blackbird nest! I wonder if there are any eggs inside?

TWEET

Bird's Nest

Birds build nests to make safe places for their eggs and young. Different birds make different kinds of nest – some, like the blackbird, make a **cup nest**.

They start by layering twigs to make a base. Then, using their beaks and feet, they weave thin, bendy sticks and grasses over and under each other into a circular shape.

Some birds stuff the gaps with mud and spider silk to stick everything together and make it stronger. Finally, the blackbird lines the nest with grass and mud to make it cosy!

Little terns don't build nests at all! Instead, they scrape a small dip in the sand or pebbles on the beach and lay their eggs. The patterns on the shells helps *camouflage* or hide them in their surroundings.

I can see the beach! Shall we go rock-pooling?

On the Beach

I LOVE the beach. Come on, let's build sandcastles!
Sand really does get everywhere, doesn't it?
But where does it all come from?

Sand

Most sand is teeny, tiny pieces of rock that have been broken down by moving water and wind over loooong periods of time.

Look in the distance. Can you see the big cliff and the waves smashing into it?

Now, imagine what happens to the cliff over thousands and millions of years. The sea and wind will slowly break the rocks into much smaller bits.

Rocks fall into rivers

Waves break up rocks

But sand's journey doesn't always start on the coast. It often begins inland, where rocks tumble into rivers and streams. Over time, the constant flow of water carries them towards the ocean, breaking them down along the way. When they arrive, the waves and tides knock the rocks and pebbles against each other, wearing them down even more until they get washed ashore as sand.

CRASH!

But not ALL sand is the result of broken-down rocks.

Black sand can start out as volcanic lava.

Shells from crabs, sea snails and clams wash up on shore and get crushed into smaller, sand-sized pieces.

Watch out! The waves might wash away our sandcastle. Where do you think waves come from?

White sand is actually parrotfish poo! The fish use their 'beaks' to scrape algae off the surface of rocks and dead corals. They grind it up, digest the good stuff, and poo out the leftover material as sand!

So the next time you build a sandcastle, just think – you're probably hands-deep in the remains of million-year-old rocks, crab shells and parrotfish poo. Yuck!

Waves

Most waves are caused by the wind blowing across the ocean's surface, making ripples. As it continues to blow, the ripples get bigger and turn into waves. The faster and harder the wind blows, the bigger the waves will be!

A wave is the movement of energy from one place to another. When energy from the wind hits the surface of the ocean, some of it passes into the water, causing water beneath the surface to move around in a circular motion. This pushes the water next to it, and the water next to it, and so on for miles – until the waves reach the beach.

Wind

Seabed

Beach

As the wave nears the shore, the water at the bottom of the wave's circle hits the seabed, which slows the movement of energy down. But the top of the wave's circle keeps moving at the same speed – forming an arched shape. This causes the top of the wave to 'break' and crash into the shore.

CRASH!

Look! There's a hermit crab walking along the beach.

Hermit Crabs

Did you know that hermit crabs aren't born with a complete shell? We don't often see it, but the lower part of their body is actually soft and curled!

Without a shell of their own to protect them, the hermit crab has to borrow old shells from other animals. They pull the curly part of their body deep inside the new shell and hook themselves in.

But they don't keep one shell for life. As they grow, they have to find a bigger one.

Sometimes, when a new shell washes ashore, hermit crabs will queue up, biggest to smallest. The biggest crab moves into the new shell, passing down its old one to the next biggest, until every hermit crab has a new, hand-me-down home!

The sun is setting. Let's go back to camp and get cosy.

Stargazing

It's a beautiful, clear night here at the campsite – perfect for stargazing! Let's snuggle up and see what we can find with the binoculars.

Binoculars

Binoculars are made of two **barrels** connected by a **hinge** – a piece of metal that connects moving parts. Inside each barrel is a set of **lenses** and **prisms**. Prisms are pieces of glass with lots of flat sides.

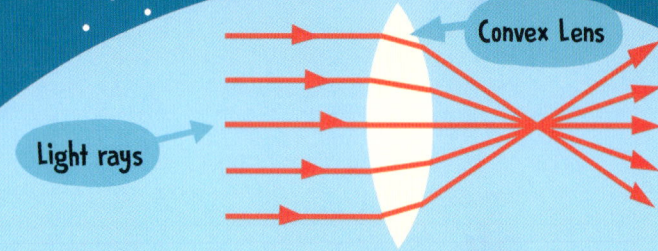

Convex Lens

Light rays

The lenses at the end of each barrel collect rays of light reflecting off a faraway object. Each lens is thicker in the middle and thinner round the edge. We call this a **convex lens**.

When light rays enter a convex lens, they bend towards the middle and are focused on to a small point. This makes the image appear bigger. But the light rays also cross over, which turns the image upside down!

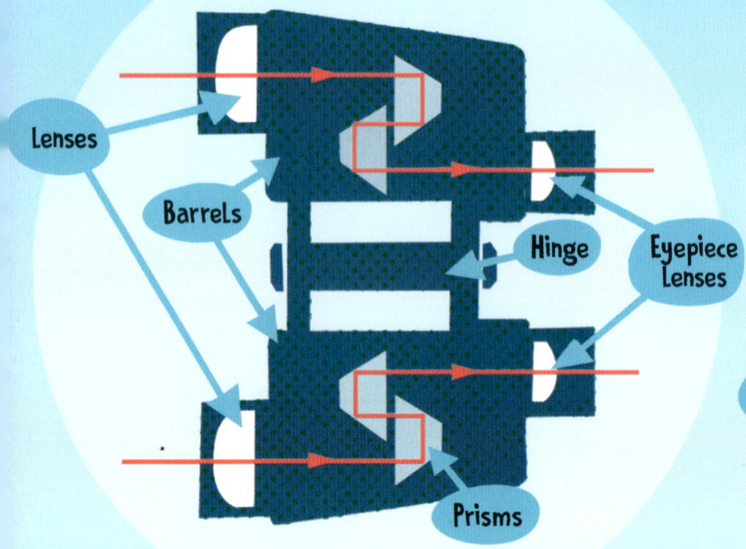

To fix this, the light rays travel down the barrel and pass through a pair of prisms. The light rays bounce off the different sides of the prisms and change direction, causing the image to be flipped again so that it's the right way up.

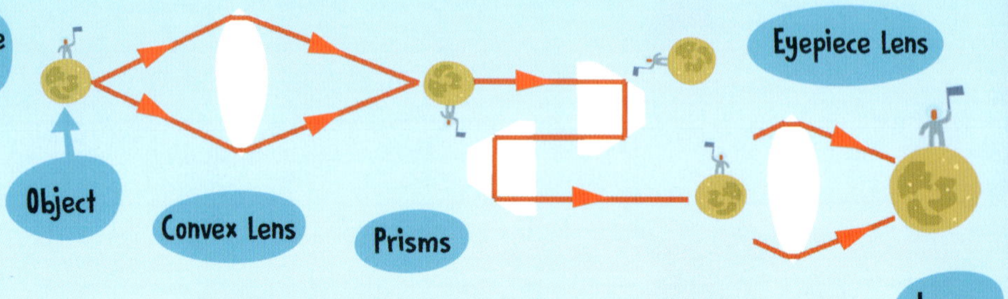

Lenses

Barrels

Hinge

Eyepiece Lenses

Prisms

Object

Convex Lens

Prisms

Eyepiece Lens

Image

Finally, the light rays travel through a second, smaller convex lens called the **eyepiece**. The eyepiece focuses the image on to a small point behind the lens, which is where we look through the binoculars.

This makes the image bigger again, and allows us to see objects that are far away, like the Moon, in much more detail.

Did you know that the Sun is a star? It's the centre of our *solar system* – which includes the Sun and all the planets and space objects that *orbit* (or travel around) it. Some of the other dots in the dark sky are distant stars that are *light years* away. One light year is the distance light travels in a year – about 6 trillion miles!

Thousands of years ago, people started drawing imaginary lines to create pictures between groups of stars. We call these *constellations*. Astronomers, who study the stars, still use constellations today to navigate the night sky. Let's play astronomers and try spotting some constellations ourselves!

Constellation Map

| Ursa Major | Ursa Minor | Hercules | Pegasus | Orion's belt | Taurus | Leo | Cassiopeia |

Great job, campers. What a sparkling end to our adventures. Now, it's time to curl up in our cosy sleeping bags and get some rest. Goodnight all!

Things You Might Want to Know!

In this book, we've learned a lot about how things work - from waves to wind turbines and more! Almost everything we've learned about in this book can be described as *matter*. But what is matter?

States of Matter

Matter is basically any stuff that takes up space, and it's made up of tiny pieces we can't see called molecules. Molecules are made of smaller building blocks called atoms, and atoms are made of EVEN SMALLER bits, some of which are called *protons* and electrons!

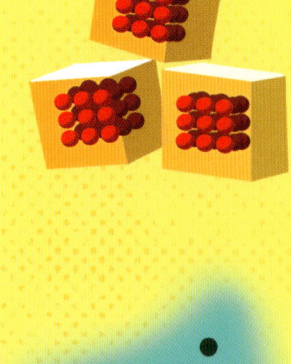

All matter can be a solid, a liquid, or a gas – we call these the three states of matter:

Solids can be hard like a rock or soft like a sock, small as a grain of sand or as big as the Moon! What makes them all solid is that their atoms are tightly locked together so they hold their shape.

Liquids, on the other hand, are flowy. Their atoms are held together less tightly, so they can move around and slide past each other. This is why you can pour liquids into any shape of container.

Gases are often invisible to our eyes, but they are still made of atoms. The atoms are really spread out and full of energy, whizzing around in all directions.

Sometimes, the state of matter of an object or substance can change. When water gets heated up past a certain point, it turns into a gas called water vapour. This process is called evaporation. When the water vapour cools down again, it turns back into liquid water – this is called condensation.

Electricity

There is one thing I've mentioned a lot in this book that isn't a solid, a liquid OR a gas – electricity! We often describe electricity as a 'flow of energy', but what does that mean?

Remember protons and electrons? The tiny particles that help make up an atom.

An electron has what is called a negative charge.

A proton has a positive charge.

A neutron has no charge at all.

Positive and negative charges try to pull each other together, or attract, each other. But two positive charges or two negative charges try to push each other away, or *repel*, each other. An electric current is created when electrons get pushed and pulled between atoms, so that they flow from one place to another.

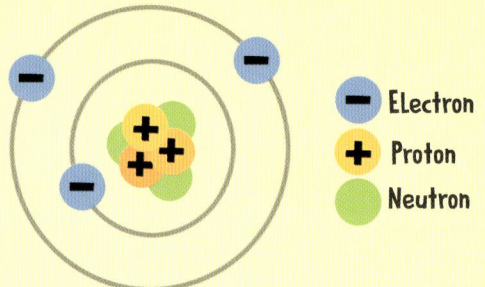

- **–** Electron
- **+** Proton
- Neutron

ATTRACT

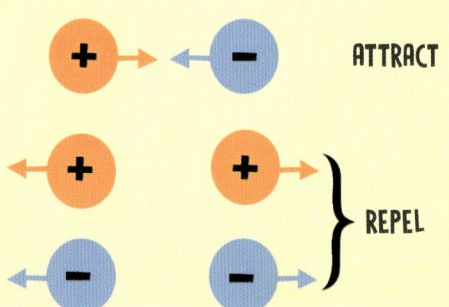

REPEL

An electric current is created when electrons get pushed and pulled between atoms, so that they flow from one place to another.

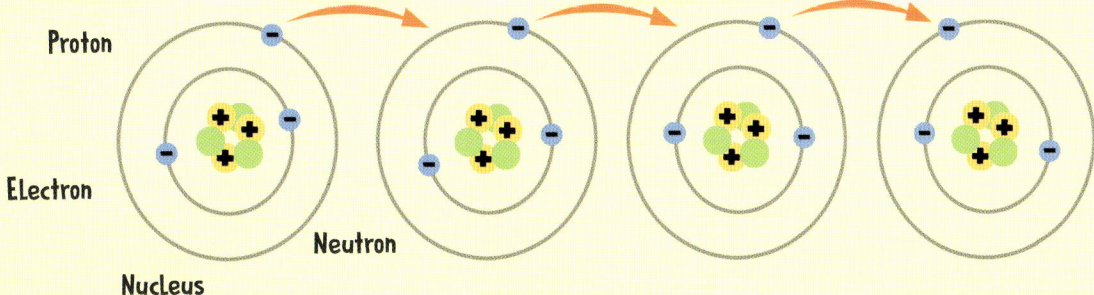

Proton

Electron

Neutron

Nucleus

How do Electric Circuits Work?

A simple electric circuit is made up of a power source – such as a battery – that is connected by wires to an electrical device, such as a lightbulb. A battery has a negative end and a positive end. The electrons flow from the negative end, which repels them, and travel along the wire to the positive end, which attracts them.

Electricity can only flow through a circuit where there are no gaps. If you have a switch in your circuit and you turn the switch to 'open' (or off), it creates a gap in the circuit, which stops the electric current from flowing. When you turn the switch to 'closed' (or on) it closes the gap, so the current can flow round the circuit again.

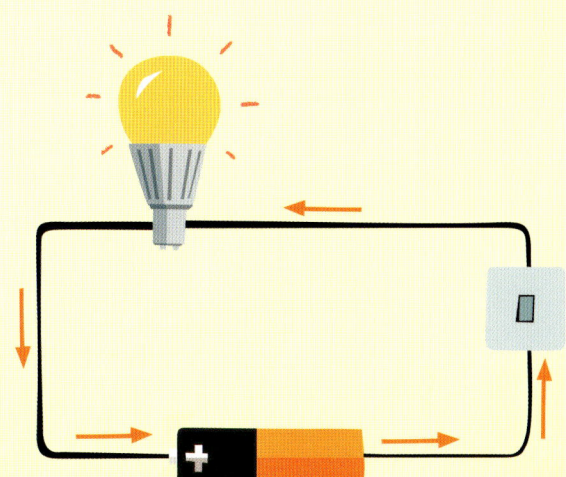

Lots of the electronic devices you have seen in this book contain circuit boards. These have different parts of a circuit attached to a flat base, which is made from material that doesn't allow electricity to pass through it. So the electric current can flow round the circuit, but not the base. The circuit boards inside electrical devices – like a smart speakers! – send the current where it needs to go to power the device.

Electric Generators

Most of the electricity that we use to power our homes comes from power stations that create electricity using generators. Generators have a spinning part called a rotor that moves a **coil of wire** past a **magnet**. The positive end of the magnet attracts electrons and the negative end repels them, which pushes and pulls the electrons round the wire, creating electricity.

Generators use kinetic energy – or the energy of motion – to drive the spinning rotor. In a wind **turbine**, for example, the kinetic energy comes from the wind spinning the turbine's blades!

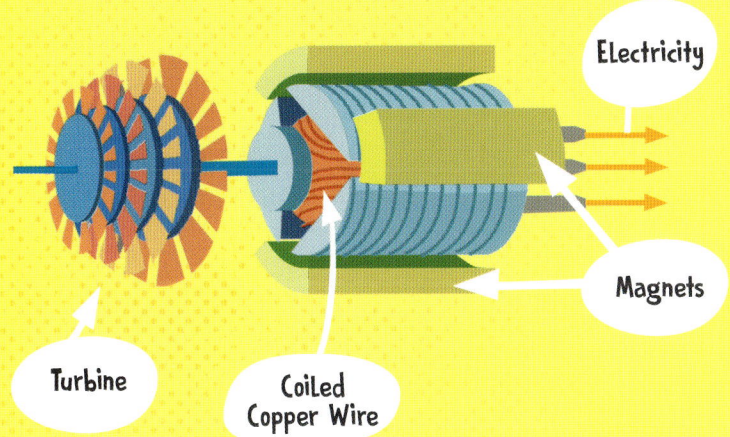

Electricity

Magnets

Turbine

Coiled Copper Wire

The electricity travels from power stations to our homes through a network of wires and pylons (big triangular structures that hold up the wires!) called the electric grid.

Electric motors work in a similar way to generators, but in reverse: in a motor, the electric current causes the magnet to move back and forth, which in turn makes the rotor spin! (Flip back to page 47 to see inside an electric car motor.)

Glossary

Here you can find some handy definitions for some of the technical words that I've used throughout this book.
It's always fun to learn new words that help us understand how things work!

STAY CURIOUS!

Acid
An acid is a substance that tastes sour when it's in a watery mixture. Lemon juice and vinegar are both acids. However, really strong acids should never be tasted or touched because they can burn and irritate our skin. The opposite of an acid is known as an alkali. Baking soda and washing-up liquid are both alkalis.

Atoms
Atoms are the basic building blocks of matter, and are made of even smaller particles called electrons, protons and neutrons. When atoms are joined with other atoms they form molecules. A substance that is made up of all the same kinds of atom – such as hydrogen or oxygen – is known as an element. An element cannot be broken down into any other substance, and every element is made of only one kind of atom.

Bacteria
Bacteria are tiny living things found almost everywhere on Earth. They are made of a single cell and can usually only be seen through a microscope.

Camouflage
Camouflage is a way of hiding something by covering or colouring it so that it looks like its surroundings. Many animals, including tigers and giraffes, use camouflage to help protect themselves, as the patterns on their bodies help them blend in with their environment and makes them difficult to spot.

Capillary action
Capillary action happens when a liquid flows in a narrow space – such as a straw – without the help of any outside forces. With capillary action, liquids can even flow upwards against the downward pull of gravity!

Cavities
A cavity is another word for a hole or a hollow place. Cavities can be found everywhere, but we often talk about the ones in our teeth. They happen when a build-up of bacteria eats away at your tooth enamel, causing a hole. That's why it's important to always brush your teeth.

Chemical reactions
A chemical is made up of one or more elements. Some chemicals, like water, can be found in nature, while others are made in factories and laboratories. A chemical reaction happens when one or more chemicals are changed into one or more other chemicals.

Circuit board
A circuit board is a flat base with electronic parts attached to it. The different electronic parts are usually connected by thin lines of metal creating a path that electricity can flow through.

Condense
To condense something is to make it denser, meaning to squeeze its atoms closer together. When water vapour condenses it becomes a liquid, and we call this process condensation.

Constellations
Constellations are groups of stars that create a recognizable pattern in the night sky. They are usually named after the thing they look like or characters from myths and legends, such as 'The Plough' or 'Hercules'.

Database
A database is a collection of data – or information – that is stored and organized (usually by a computer).

Density
Density is the measure of how much 'stuff' is in a given amount of space. The more atoms that are squeezed into a space, the denser it becomes.

Displacement
When one type of matter pushes another out of its original container or location, such as water pushing air out of a bottle as it is filled.

Electric grid
The electric grid is a system that connects generating stations (places that generate electricity) to our homes through underground cables, overhead power lines and pylons.

Electrical circuit
An electric circuit is a loop of connected electrical parts that electricity can flow through.

Electromagnetic spectrum
Scientists use the electromagnetic spectrum to describe all the different types of light. It contains radio waves, visible light, microwaves, and even X-rays. Most of the light on the electromagnetic spectrum is invisible to us.

Electrons
An electron is a very small particle found in an atom. It has a negative charge.

Enamel
Enamel is a word for a smooth, shiny coating that protects different things, including our teeth! Tooth enamel is very strong – in fact, it's the hardest material in your body.

Evaporate
To evaporate means to turn from a liquid into a gas. When water is heated up, it evaporates and becomes water vapour.

Focus

The point at which rays of light or heat come together, or from which they move away. Sometimes we might adjust – or 'focus' – a device, such as a microscope or a pair of binoculars, to give us a clearer image of the thing we are looking at through a lens.

Force

A force is a type of push or pull that either changes or keeps the motion of an object the same. Forces can change an object's speed, direction, and even its shape.

Friction

Friction is a force created when two surfaces rub or try to move across each other. A rougher surface causes more friction than something smooth. The more friction, the tougher it is for those surfaces to move against each other.

Gluten

Gluten is a type of protein found in wheat that works a bit like glue to hold things together and give them stretch.

Gravity

An invisible force that pulls objects towards each other. On Earth, gravity is the force that pulls things towards the centre of our planet and causes objects to fall to the ground.

Insulation

An insulator is a material that does not easily allow heat and/or electricity to pass through it.

Light year

A light year is the distance light travels in one year.

Matter

Matter is all the stuff that makes up our world – including solids, liquids and gases. Matter can describe anything that takes up space and is made up of atoms.

Molecules

A molecule is a particle made up of two or more atoms that have joined together.

Neutron

A neutron is another very small particle found in the centre of an atom. It has no charge.

Orbit

An orbit is the path of an object round a central point – for example, the path the Moon takes around the Earth.

Phosphorescence

Phosphorescence is the glowing light that some types of molecules give off after they have soaked up light energy.

Phosphors

Phosphors are a type of molecule that glow with visible light after they have absorbed certain types of light energy.

Photons

A photon is a tiny particle made up of electromagnetic waves. You can think of them as miniature bundles of light energy.

Photovoltaic cells

A photovoltaic cell is a device that collects light energy and changes it into electrical energy.

Proton

A proton is a very small particle found in an atom. It has a positive charge.

Radiation

Radiation is energy that can move from one place to another through empty space. Visible light, sound, heat and X-rays are all types of radiation.

Radio waves

Radio waves are a type of light that we can't see. They are the electromagnetic waves with the longest wavelength and are used to carry information to and from radios and satellites.

Repel

In science, the word 'repel' describes two things pushing away from each other.

Semiconductor

A semiconductor is a material that helps control the flow of electricity.

Shearing

Shearing is the action of cutting and clipping hair or wool with a tool. For example, a farmer might shear a sheep with a set of clippers to remove its wool.

Solar system

A solar system is a group of planets, moons, asteroids, comets and the star they orbit.

Sound-wave

All sounds are made by a vibrating object. Those vibrations disturb the molecules around them. These molecules then bump into the molecules close to them, which makes them vibrate too, causing them to bump into more molecules. This movement is called a sound-wave, and it may eventually travel all the way to your ear for you to hear!

Vibrate

When something vibrates it moves back and forward really, really quickly. We call these tiny movements vibrations.

ANSWERS

RACETRACK – Page 19

SPOT THE DIFFERENCE – Page 31

WORD LADDER – Page 43

CAT
PAT
PAD
POD
ROD
RED

STARGAZING – Page 55

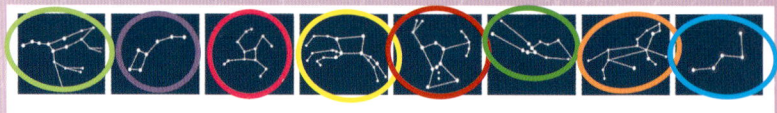

THINGS TO SPOT!

Finding things can be really exciting, especially when you notice something new –
like a tiny mini-beast under a leaf or a star in the sky. Sometimes you
might even find something no one else has ever seen before!

See if you can spot these things in the book. What else can you find?

Keep exploring!

Spider

Mouse

Copy of *A Very Curious Christmas*

Nigel the Yeti

Puddles the Penguin

Llamas

Pirate flag

Tooth-shaped clock

Fish tank on wheels

Snake in a box

Bag of cat treats

Camping Lantern

Sailing boat

Statue of Liberty

Surfer

And see if you can spot me throughout the book too!